SUZANNE DE PASSE

Motown's
Boss
Lady

SUZANNE DE PASSE

Motown's Boss Lady

Mark Mussari

GEC **GARRETT EDUCATIONAL CORPORATION**

Cover: *Suzanne de Passe.* (Steve Smith.)

Copyright © 1992 by Mark Mussari

All rights reserved including the right of reproduction in whole or in part in any form without the prior written permission of the publisher. Published by Garrett Educational Corporation, 130 East 13th Street, P.O. Box 1588, Ada, Oklahoma 74820.

Manufactured in the United States of America

Edited and produced by Synthegraphics Corporation

Library of Congress Cataloging in Publication Data

Mussari, Mark.
   Suzanne de Passe : Motown's boss lady / Mark Mussari.
     p. cm. — (Wizards of business)
   Includes index.
   Summary: A biography of the president of Motown Productions, a bright, determined woman whose business gifts have brought her many awards in television and movie production.
   ISBN 1-56074-026-4
   1. De Passe, Suzanne, 1947-   —Juvenile literature.   2. Sound recording executives and producers—United States—Biography—Juvenile literature.   3. Women in business—United States—Biography—Juvenile literature.   4. Sound recording industry—United States—Juvenile literature.   5. Motown Record Corporation—Juvenile literature.   [1. De Passe, Suzanne, 1947-
2. Television producers and directors.   3. Motion picture producers and directors.   4. Afro-Americans—Biography.   5. Gordy, Berry.]
I. Title.   II. Series.
HD9697.P562D436   1991
782.42116'092—dc20   91-28541
[B]   CIP
                                                                 AC

Contents

Chronology for **Suzanne de Passe**	6
Chapter **1** *Taking Care of Business*	7
Chapter **2** *Beginnings*	19
Chapter **3** *Hard Work and Determination*	27
Chapter **4** *The Supreme Challenge*	33
Chapter **5** *Motown Productions*	41
Chapter **6** *Lonesome Dove*	51
Chapter **7** *Lady in Control*	57
Glossary	61
Index	63

Chronology for Suzanne de Passe

1947 — Born on July 19 in the Harlem section of New York City

1966 — Attended Syracuse University and Manhattan Community College; worked as Talent Coordinator for the Cheetah discotheque in New York City

1968 — Hired in January as Creative Assistant to Berry Gordy, president of Motown Records

1970 — Became head of Motown's Talent and Acquisitions Department

1972 — Co-authored screenplay for *Lady Sings the Blues*; nominated for an Academy Award

1978 — Married actor Paul Le Mat

1979 — Became vice-president of Motown Productions

1981 — Became president of Motown Productions

1983 — Produced *Motown 25*; won her first Emmy Award and a Peabody Award

1985 — Produced *Motown Returns to the Apollo*; won second Emmy Award

1989 — Produced *Lonesome Dove*, a TV mini-series that won seven Emmy Awards.

Chapter 1

Taking Care of Business

Suzanne de Passe was angry.

For weeks the young black woman had tried to get in touch with someone at Motown Records. She was working as a booking agent, someone who signs performers to appear in concert. After all, the Motown recording label had all the great singing groups of the 1960s: The Supremes, The Temptations, The Four Tops, Smokey Robinson and The Miracles.

De Passe wanted to sign some of these superstars to appear at her company's music halls. Her bosses owned many popular concert sites, including the famous Westbury Music Fair near New York City. As hard as she tried, de Passe just couldn't get anywhere. No one at Motown returned her calls; no dates could be confirmed for the acts.

Suzanne de Passe was annoyed. She knew that this was no way to run a business.

Luckily, however, she had a connection. One of her best friends was Cindy Birdsong, from Camden, New Jersey. Birdsong had recently joined The Supremes, the most successful black female singing group in recording history. The Supremes were the most popular Motown act of all time.

A CHANCE MEETING

When her friend Cindy invited her to a New Year's Eve party in 1967, de Passe couldn't wait. At the party she ran into Berry Gordy, a black **entrepreneur** who was the president and founder of Motown Records. (Terms in **boldface type** are defined in the Glossary at the back of this book.) She had met him once before, but only briefly.

De Passe still remembers their conversation at that party: "I purposely went up to him and said, 'You know, I have a very important job to do, and it's impossible to do that job because the people in your company can't even give a lousy answer about an act.'"

Berry Gordy was surprised at the young woman's anger and criticism. He told her he didn't know what the problem was with his company. He also told her he could use someone like de Passe to help straighten things out. De Passe couldn't believe her ears. "I just melted into the carpet," she said.

Three weeks later, Suzanne de Passe became Gordy's Creative Assistant. She would work closely with him on all aspects of the recording business, but she would especially help him with developing new talent. He knew that this was her special gift. "I liked

Suzanne de Passe, president of Gordy/de Passe Productions, in 1987, on the set of Nightlife, *one of her many television projects.* (Benno Friedman.)

her honest approach," Gordy has recalled. "And I liked the fact that she was a historian of the Motown sound."

A Creative Talent

Gordy soon discovered that de Passe knew as much about his famous acts as he did. Impressed with this determined, bright young woman, he wanted to create special opportunities just for her in his company. He knew talent when he saw it.

Gordy also knew he would need de Passe's talent for his future plans. Soon, Motown—a company that had only produced hit records—would be branching out into new areas, especially television and movies. In time, Suzanne de Passe's intelligence and business instincts would lead to her position as vice-president of Motown Productions, the part of Motown that creates television series and films.

In 1981, de Passe became president of Motown Productions—now known as Gordy/de Passe Productions—and she still holds that impressive post. Today, she is the power behind this $65 million production company.

Along the way, de Passe has achieved incredible success. It has never been easy for a woman or a black person to break into the business side of the film and television industry. For a black woman to have done so is unheard of. But Berry Gordy believed in the strong, young lady who told him off at that New Year's Eve party in 1967. He knew she was a winner.

Today, Suzanne de Passe realizes that the odds were against her. She was a woman *and* she was black. She had to make it in a business dominated by white men.

Still, de Passe never let that stop her. "It's not that you never notice these things, but it's how you handle them," she once explained. "You have to keep your mind on what is truly most important, and that's the work."

THE MOTOWN STORY

When Suzanne de Passe received her first job with Motown Records in 1968, she joined a recording company with a rich and exciting history. There had never been anything like Motown.

It seems only fitting that a black woman would make such an incredible name for herself with a company that had created great opportunities for black talent. For most black performers, many of these opportunities had never existed before Motown.

Berry Gordy, the founder and former president of Motown Records. Gordy has been a pioneer in the field of contemporary music and is credited with mass-marketing rhythm and blues to a broader audience. (Gordy/de Passe Productions.)

A Man with a Dream

In 1958, Berry Gordy—the man who started Motown—borrowed $800 because he had a dream. Gordy had been a successful boxer and a winner of the Golden Gloves Award. Music, however, was his first love. He dreamed of making hit records.

By the late 1950s, rock and roll music had taken America by storm. It was still new and exciting. Black music, however—especially **rhythm and blues**—was still thought of as "race music" (music only for black people).

Gordy believed that *all* music, from blues to pop to country, could be enjoyed by everyone. He wanted to create a new recording label—a company that would bring rhythm and blues to both black *and* white listeners.

With the $800 he borrowed from his family, Gordy rented a small building in Detroit, Michigan, and called it "Hitsville, U.S.A." He set up a recording studio, hired musicians, and searched to discover the best talent he could find in the Detroit area.

Most people still think of Detroit as the automobile capital of the United States. In fact, it has always been called "Motor Town," because so many cars are manufactured there. Motown is another name for Motor Town, and that is the name Gordy chose for his recording company.

Actually, Gordy had worked for Ford Motor Company, one of the world's largest manufacturers of cars. At Ford, Gordy learned about **assembly-line** production. Each step along the way to making a new car added something important and special. Gordy felt that he could apply this approach to music.

Making Hit Records

After he signed a number of musicians and singers to his new label, Gordy created his own assembly line for making hit records and superstars. He called it "artistic development." Gordy described this process as "the grooming of the act, how to talk, how to speak, how to walk. And when you got through . . . you were a star, a potential star. It was that assembly-line approach to things."

The singers all dressed in the same outfits, which they jokingly called "uniforms." This became a trademark of the great Motown groups of the 1960s. People knew when they saw The Temptations or The Supremes that they would all be dressed alike. It helped listeners to identify the groups.

Gordy rehearsed the groups for long, hard hours every day. The Temptations did so much dancing on stage while they sang that

The Production of Stars

> Production is taking resources and turning them into goods and services. Berry Gordy had people—*natural* resources—to work with, and he wanted to turn them into stars. Many of the acts he signed to recording contracts needed to develop their talents. To do this, Gordy used the assembly-line procedure he had learned while working at Ford Motor Company.
>
> Gordy created polished professionals after the singers and musicians passed through his "artistic development" assembly line. In a way, he treated his performers like a product that had to be molded into just the right shape before it is sent out to the public. He *produced* stars out of ordinary people.

they had to practice up to eleven hours a day before a performance. Young people everywhere began to imitate their difficult dance steps.

Musically, Gordy tried many new styles to achieve that special Motown sound. Sometimes, he added violins to the records, giving the rhythm and blues numbers the sound of a symphony orchestra in the background. If a certain rhythm were needed, he might have someone clapping boards of wood together (as in the beginning of The Supremes' "Where Did Our Love Go?"), or he might have someone stomping on a chair (as in The Four Tops' hit "Reach Out").

Gordy also had an incredible eye for spotting talent. Mary Wilson, one of the original Supremes, says that he could look at someone and immediately know what that person did well. And he took chances.

For example, Gordy hired a young, blind singer and musician named Stevie Wonder when he was only twelve years old. Today, Stevie Wonder—who still sings for Motown—is considered a musical genius.

That Motown Sound

Gordy could never have imagined how successful his Motown label would become. He sent his talented performers on tours all over the country to promote their records. The tour bus might have held Stevie Wonder, The Four Tops, Marvin Gaye, and Martha and the Vandellas—all appearing together in concert. Young people everywhere—black and white—could not get enough of this new form of rhythm and blues.

By the beginning of the 1960s, songs such as The Miracles' "Shop Around" and The Marvelettes' "Please, Mr. Postman" could be heard on radio stations all over the United States. Today, these early Motown tunes are considered classic rock and roll songs. Even the Beatles, who recorded three Motown songs on their second album, were influenced by the Motown sound.

The company called its special brand of music "The Sound of Young America." Most people, however, called it "Soul." Throughout the 1960s, Motown songs topped the music charts all over the world.

The Motown groups began to appear on network television shows and at clubs and concert halls all around the country. Many

The original Temptations, one of the many Motown acts to top the record charts: from left, Paul Williams, Eddie Kendricks, Melvin Franklin, David Ruffin, and Otis Williams. Their unique harmonies and polished dance steps made them the greatest male vocal group of the 1960s. (Michael Ochs Archives.)

obstacles that previously had stood in the way of black performers disappeared. And their music became popular with both young and old people. Motown was a musical revolution. It changed forever the way people looked at black performers.

Berry Gordy's dream of great music for *everyone* had become a reality.

Someone once asked Gordy to define the Motown sound. What was it? What made it so unique? He replied, "Rats, roaches, guts, and love." The sound was joyful and made people feel happy—and it still does today.

A Lasting Influence

In the 1990s, many movies, television shows, and commercials use old Motown songs because of their special quality. And performers like Billy Joel, Phil Collins, and Madonna have talked frequently about the influence of Motown on their music.

The lesson of Motown is really quite simple. Gordy gave rhythm and blues some class—and class never goes out of style. During Motown's first sixteen years, Gordy earned an unbelievable $367 million. "I didn't want to be a big record **mogul**," Gordy has said. "I just wanted to write songs and make people laugh."

BRANCHING OUT

At first, Motown was only a record company. Gordy spent all of his time working with performers he knew would achieve the greatest popularity: superstars like The Supremes and The Temptations. Their success on the music charts and in concert paved the way for Motown to branch out into television and films.

By 1967, when Gordy first met Suzanne de Passe, he was already thinking about new possibilities for his constantly growing company. In the trio of black women known as The Supremes—and especially their lead singer, Diana Ross—Gordy saw potential for recording stars to do television specials and movies. He knew that Ross was talented enough to do anything.

The Supremes broke all barriers that had once stood in the way of many black performers. They appeared at all the best concert halls and nightclubs. Everywhere they went they would break attendance records. They performed before royalty and with big-name entertainers on television. They had more number one records than anyone except the Beatles and Elvis Presley.

In 1967, Gordy decided it was time to try something different with The Supremes. He wanted them to have their own television special. He was sure that Diana Ross would become a big star—a superstar—and he knew that television would be the perfect beginning for her solo career.

Motown would soon branch out into television and film as Motown Productions. But to do so, Berry Gordy was going to need some help.

Chapter 2

Beginnings

Two months went by after Berry Gordy first hired Suzanne de Passe in 1968. During this time, nothing happened. She just sat in Gordy's New York office and collected her paychecks from Motown. Confused, she finally called Gordy in Detroit, where Motown had its headquarters. "Have you forgotten me?" she asked him.

"What do you think I am, stupid?" Gordy replied. "You think you're not worth waiting for? When I have something for you to do, I'll let you know." More time went by. Then one day Gordy called de Passe with her first assignment. She was to watch Smokey Robinson and The Miracles perform and criticize their act.

De Passe couldn't believe it. Only a few weeks before, she was standing in line—with everyone else—at the Apollo Theater in the Harlem section of New York City. (All the great black performers appeared at the Apollo.) Now, she would be telling one of those acts what was wrong with its show. "I said that some of it was quite corny," she remembers.

It is interesting that de Passe's first assignment from Motown was to go to the Apollo Theater. The young New York woman had grown up right there in Harlem.

A SPECIAL CHILDHOOD

Suzanne de Passe was born on July 19, 1947, to a middle-class family living in Harlem. Her family originally came from the West Indies, making her **ethnic** background West Indian. Education is very important to West Indians. Her grandfather was a doctor, and her father had been an executive with a company called Seagram's. Her mother was a schoolteacher.

When Suzanne was only three years old, her parents separated. Coming from a broken home can be difficult for most children, but de Passe's situation was special. Although divorced, her parents continued to work for their daughter's well-being. When her father remarried—when Suzanne was nine—his new wife also joined in supporting the young girl.

Thus, Suzanne's close-knit family was made up of *three* parents: her mother, father, and stepmother. She recalls that her special childhood gave her "a certain security—though not financial. I was definitely aware that I was black, but I also was aware that I had ability and hope and promise."

Suzanne's parents wanted their daughter—an only child—to have the best education. So, they sent her to New Lincoln, a special private school that was integrated (one where both black and white children went to school together). De Passe remembers New Lincoln as "the place where I learned to express my opinion about things—and that's been the reason for my success."

Growing Up with Music

Suzanne's parents also tried to surround their daughter with culture. Her mother took her to the opera and to see dance groups. De Passe also remembers that her house was always filled with music. "We listened to everything from Dinah Washington to Vanilla Fudge, from calypso to reggae to the Chambers Brothers, Chicago Transit Authority, and, of course, Motown," she has recalled.

Growing up with so much music around her, Suzanne developed a good musical ear. She also developed strong opinions about what she did and didn't like. Mostly, she just plain loved music. "I'd tell my mother I was at the library," she once said, "and I'd be sitting at the Apollo Theater."

Originally, Suzanne wanted to be a writer. "I always wanted to create a novel and stories," she has recalled. "As a child I had a vivid imagination, and I still see things in pictures." This talent would work to her advantage later in life.

Suzanne spent her summers with wealthy black children in a town called Oak Bluffs, on Martha's Vineyard, an island off the coast of Massachusetts. There, she developed her skill in horseback riding. Her parents made sure she had only the best. Mostly, they wanted her to be a great scholar.

De Passe, on the other hand, wanted to be someone special: "I absolutely pictured myself climbing in and out of limousines."

A Mind of Her Own

The de Passes' daughter had a mind all her own. In 1966, she started to attend Syracuse University. She then transferred to Manhattan Community College, so that she could live in New York City. Suzanne liked the New York nightlife better than the academic world, however. That same year (1966), at the age of 19, she dropped out of college.

"I was a night person who loved to dance," she remembers. And she also loved her motorcycle—a Honda 250—and speeding down New York's Park Avenue at four in the morning.

Her father was greatly disappointed when he heard that Suzanne had left school. "Coming from the West Indian tradition of emphasizing education, he couldn't understand what I was doing," de Passe recalls. Later in life, she said she regretted not getting her degree. Still, she knew that her talents could be used somewhere else: "I knew I was destined to do something in entertainment."

RECOGNIZING TALENT

One of the places where Suzanne would go a couple of nights each week was the Cheetah, a popular discotheque (dance club) in New York. She danced at the disco, and she seemed to have a keen ear for identifying musical talent.

"I'd let the management know what I liked and disliked," Suzanne remembers. "I would say, 'This band is really lousy—no fun to dance to, and so on, or this band is great.'" The owners of the disco couldn't help but listen to this bright young woman with smart musical instincts.

At first, the owners invited Suzanne to sit in on talent auditions and offer her "official" opinion. She earned only $25 a week for her troubles. She called herself "the last living authority on live music in New York City."

The Cheetah's owners liked what they heard from de Passe. In fact, they liked it so much that they soon hired her as Talent Coordinator for the dance club. Suzanne quickly learned all aspects of the business: signing contracts, performer percentages, union wages, and the like. Part of her job was booking talent for the disco.

Help from a Friend

It was at this time in Suzanne's life that she became friendly with Cindy Birdsong of The Supremes. That friendship led to her meeting with Berry Gordy at the New Year's Eve party in Florida, where she told him that his company (Motown Records) was poorly managed.

In reality, Suzanne had met Gordy once before—very briefly. Her job at the Cheetah meant many late hours for de Passe. Sometimes, she found it hard to get a taxi in New York at early hours in the morning. When many of the cab drivers saw she was black—and probably going to Harlem—they would drive off.

Suzanne solved this problem in the only way she knew how. At great expense—eight dollars an hour—she would rent a limousine. In a way, de Passe had been forced into fulfilling one of her childhood dreams: to ride in a limousine.

24 *Suzanne de Passe*

The Supremes, Motown's most successful recording group, broke down all barriers with their talent and glamour. Shown here in 1968, Diana Ross (sitting) is flanked by Cindy Birdsong, left, and Mary Wilson, right. It was Birdsong who first introduced Suzanne de Passe to Berry Gordy. (Michael Ochs Archives.)

One night, Suzanne rented a limo and went to pick up Cindy Birdsong, who had just finished rehearsing with The Supremes for a television appearance on *The Ed Sullivan Show*. "Cindy came out and said, 'Berry Gordy's car hasn't come, can we give him a ride?' I said, 'Sure.' So the first time I met Berry, I gave him a ride in my limousine."

When they met again almost a year later at the New Year's Eve party, Gordy remembered the beautiful woman who had offered him a ride. He immediately saw a special talent in de Passe: "She had so much style and such great taste, and that one-step ahead quality of hers helped Motown keep up its high standards."

Chapter 3

Hard Work and Determination

After spending two months in Gordy's New York office, Suzanne de Passe moved to Detroit to work at Motown. She knew right from the start that the job wasn't going to be easy. She had to overcome many barriers. "I belonged in Detroit like a fish belongs on a bike," she once said.

Some of the people who had been with Motown for a long time resented her. Who was this young newcomer who had already become a Creative Assistant? Many thought she was just one of Gordy's girl friends. But she was determined to show them they were wrong.

MEETING THE CHALLENGE

Surprisingly, one of Suzanne's greatest problems was her boss: Gordy seemed determined to make life tough for de Passe. She knew he was doing it on purpose, however. Even with many of his most talented songwriters—like Smokey Robinson—Gordy would reject their songs just to make them try harder.

"Even as I rejected every song, Smokey got stronger," Gordy once explained. "That's the mark of a real winner." It was his style of management, and de Passe knew she would have to work with it.

Working for a Bear

But Suzanne would not give up; she decided to "rise to the challenge." Looking back, she now sees that Gordy let her "mess up a lot of things." She knows that he "spent a lot of money" on her early years with the company. But they both knew it would pay off.

Gordy admits, "I've been strict with Suzanne, and there were ten years of tears, but I believe competition breeds champions." Today, he says that he doesn't know "who's the teacher and who's the pupil anymore—and I don't really care."

Many years later, de Passe looked back on her learning period at Motown in a different light: "I think Berry Gordy is a genius, and it's not a word I throw around lightly. But with all that comes the **idiosyncratic** behavior of a self-made, talented, creative person, and that's not easy to come up against. It's not that he would never listen, but he was kind of like a bear coming through the woods—crash, crash, crash."

AN EYE FOR TALENT

De Passe felt that she had to prove herself to everyone around her at Motown. To do so, she worked long hours in the recording studio and learned everything about making a hit record. She went on tours with the performers, taking notes on each show and criticizing their acts.

In her book *Dreamgirl: My Life as a Supreme*, Mary Wilson recalls that de Passe was always with The Supremes and Gordy—and always writing something down, looking for ways to improve the group.

De Passe also acquired management skills. She managed the career of a number of stars, including Billy Preston, a talented keyboard player who has been called "the fifth Beatle," because he played with the Beatles so often.

Some Important Discoveries

The eye for talent that de Passe had developed while working at the Cheetah disco served her well at Motown. For example, she discovered Lionel Richie, a singer who would experience incredible success later in his career. De Passe was convinced that Richie and his group, the Commodores, would someday be a big hit.

Suzanne flew all the way to an island in the Caribbean to play Richie's songs for Gordy, who was on a vacation and surprised by her visit. Because she was so strong-willed, she talked him into signing the future hit-maker. "She's a **persuasive,** determined woman," Gordy has said. Her instincts were right. Richie became a superstar.

Discovering Michael Jackson

De Passe made a special audition film of another group, five boys from Gary, Indiana, who called themselves The Jackson 5. She used that film to persuade Gordy to sign the unknown group to the

The Jackson 5, shown here in 1971, was one of the acts Suzanne de Passe convinced Berry Gordy to hire. Her intuition was right on the mark—and young Michael (second from right) has since become a superstar. (Michael Ochs Archives.)

Motown label. Needless to say, it was a smart move. Michael Jackson, the youngest of the five brothers, went on to become one of the most successful recording artists of all time.

Anthony Jones, her cousin and co-worker, has commented on de Passe's unique influence on The Jackson 5. "We rehearsed them every day," he explains, "**choreographed** their moves, shopped to give them a groovy look."

De Passe worked especially hard at giving the group—and its young lead singer, Michael Jackson—a special appearance. She even traveled with the group for a while. In 1971, de Passe wrote The Jackson 5's first television special, *Goin' Back to Indiana*.

Many years later, Michael Jackson would remember Suzanne de Passe in his autobiography, *Moonwalk*. "She really contributed a lot toward the shaping of the Jackson 5," he wrote, "and I'll never be able to thank her enough for all she did."

EARNING RESPECT

As time went on, de Passe eventually gained the respect of her boss, Berry Gordy. "I think there was a kind of chemistry between us," de Passe has explained. "There were times when I was sorry I met him—I spent a lot of years feeling I would never be able to please the man. But I'm the stubborn kind. I was convinced that I would live to hear him say, 'That's great'—with no buts."

De Passe recalls that during her first five years at Motown she was "constantly frustrated. I wanted to be told by Berry that I was doing okay, and he just doesn't give that kind of approval." Still, she kept trying. "I couldn't believe I couldn't do the job."

Looking back, de Passe realizes she was blessed with a combination of patience and **persistence.** "Whenever I felt like it wasn't going to happen, I persisted," she explains, "and whenever I felt it wasn't happening fast enough, something in me got patient."

Surviving in a Man's World

During the 1960s and most of the 1970s, women had very little power in the business world. This was especially true in the music industry. Many men made large sums of money quickly from hit records or smart deals. Music was—and in many ways still is—a business that demands great and sudden success.

De Passe would need all the strength and determination she had grown up with to survive in such a competitive world. She often found that being a woman made it even tougher: "There were times earlier when if I had been a man, I would have been making twice as much money."

The attitude toward women in management positions was not a good one. Sexism—the belief that women cannot do what men can do—created many problems for de Passe. She dealt with sexism in the only way she knew how—with "a certain sense of humor."

De Passe says that, in some ways, sexual **discrimination** was "a great advantage." Men constantly underestimated her ability. They thought that because she was a woman, she didn't know what she was doing. Therefore, she always tried to show them that she was brighter than they thought.

And that's exactly what she did.

Chapter 4

The Supreme Challenge

In 1968, Motown moved its offices from Detroit to Los Angeles, California, the entertainment capital of the world. Gordy knew that the company had to be near Hollywood if he wanted to make television specials and movies.

Motown produced its first television show in 1968. Gordy decided it would be an all-music special featuring his two most successful recording groups: Diana Ross and The Supremes, and The Temptations. Before she knew what was happening, Suzanne de Passe was swept into the world of television production.

A LESSON IN PRODUCTION

Most of us only think of show business as entertainment. We forget that it's called show *business*. There is a business side to every record, movie, play, or TV show that is made. Someone must handle the financial part of the entertainment world.

Producing a film or a television show means making a lot of deals. It's a job that involves convincing people to spend large sums of money to pay for the costs of your production. Within a year after she took her job with Motown, de Passe had to learn all aspects of this job. By 1970, she had become the head of Motown's Talent and Acquisitions Department.

"Fortunately, I got the opportunity to work on TV production throughout my career," de Passe explained in 1989. "From 1968 until now I've been able to access the production side of entertainment, from deal making to all other aspects of the business."

De Passe was involved in the production of the first Motown TV special, called *T.C.B.*, and another called *G.I.T. On Broadway*. Both specials starred Diana Ross and The Supremes and The Temptations. "I felt very comfortable in knowing how deals got made and how to work with star personalities and how television shows got to be on the screen," de Passe has explained.

In the future, her television experience would become very important to her career. In 1968, however, de Passe had no idea that she would one day be president of Motown Productions.

Working with a Superstar

While working on Motown television specials and touring with The Supremes, de Passe became friendly with Diana Ross. Ross had a special relationship with Berry Gordy. Throughout her career, he had prepared her to be a superstar. He spent more time and money on The Supremes than on any other group. Gordy knew that out of all his recording artists, Ross had the greatest chance for fame.

De Passe often found herself caught in the middle between Gordy and Ross. "It was a real nightmare," she has said. "I was a friend to her, and I was his employee." Learning to deal with famous people and their egos helped de Passe in her many dealings with stars. Today, Ross and de Passe are godmothers of each other's children and still talk on the phone.

Motown on Film

Because The Supremes' two television specials were huge successes, Gordy decided that the time had come for Diana Ross to leave the group and go on her own. One of his first projects for the rising superstar was a movie. It would be the first full-length motion picture produced by Motown.

Gordy chose the life of Billie Holliday, a legendary blues singer, as the basis for his movie. And he asked Suzanne de Passe to co-write the screenplay. The little girl from Harlem who had wanted to be a writer found that another dream had come true.

In 1972, Motown's first film, *Lady Sings the Blues,* starring Diana Ross, Billy Dee Williams, and Richard Pryor, took the box office by storm. When the time came for the Oscars, the Academy Awards given each year to the best films, Ross received a nomination for best actress. And de Passe received an Oscar nomination for screenwriting. It was one of the greatest moments of her life.

Some Hard Times

In 1975, Gordy and de Passe worked on another film for Diana Ross, *Mahogany,* the story of a young woman who wanted to become a fashion designer. As time went on, the movie became

Diana Ross as the legendary blues singer Billy Holiday in Lady Sings the Blues, Motown Production's first major motion picture. The film was released in 1972, and Suzanne de Passe received an Oscar nomination for her screenplay. (Movie Still Archives.)

increasingly difficult to make. Gordy was unhappy with the first few directors and fired them. In time, he took over complete control of the film.

At first, *Mahogany* did well at the box office, but the critics hated the movie. Their bad reviews almost ruined Motown's reputation for making good films. Unfortunately, more unsuccessful Motown films followed *Mahogany.* Some people saw this problem as being a racial one.

Black film production companies face many problems. The most important is a lack of money to support making a film. Also, film distributors—the people who send the films out to the theaters—do not always push black films. Therefore, even if black audiences like a film, they may not get many chances to see it.

Distribution of Movies

> **Distribution is selling a product. For products to sell, they must be promoted and advertised properly. Advertising convinces us to buy a product. The more we see it, the more we want it.**
>
> **When there is no—or little—distribution, a product will usually not sell well. For Motown Productions, this has sometimes been a problem with the company's films. Film distributors, those who send a movie out and make sure it is seen, failed to promote *The Wiz*. Therefore, the movie did not do well at the box office, and Motown lost money on it.**

The film The Wiz, an adaptation of the Wizard of Oz, was one of Motown Production's few financial failures. Its all-black cast featured such superstars as Diana Ross and Michael Jackson (second from left). (Movie Still Archives.)

This racial problem seriously affected the success of one of Motown Production's most expensive projects, the movie *The Wiz*. This was Motown's extravagant film version of the successful Broadway musical of the same name. Again, critics did not like this updated, black version of *The Wizard of Oz*. Many felt that Diana Ross was too old for the lead part.

Still, black audiences liked the film, which also starred Michael Jackson. They would have supported it even more if the movie had been sent to more theaters. But white distributors read the bad reviews (mostly written by white critics) and only sent the film for short runs to theaters in black neighborhoods. *The Wiz* lost more than $20 million.

Chapter 5

Motown Productions

In 1979, Gordy decided to use de Passe's talents by making her vice-president of Motown Productions, the television, film, stage, video, and cable branch of the business. He knew that this part of Motown needed help, and he knew that de Passe was just the person who could straighten things out.

Only two years later, in 1981, de Passe was named president of Motown Productions. Many of the Motown employees couldn't believe it. They still felt that de Passe was a newcomer to the company. Some even wore black clothes to protest her advancement.

DEVELOPING A MANAGEMENT STYLE

De Passe knew what she had to do. She had worked too hard to let these people hold her back. She immediately fired all of them. And she set a goal for herself. People may have thought Motown only meant music, but she would show Hollywood that Motown could do anything.

The new president of Motown Productions was going to win Hollywood over. She had to because Motown needed the financial backing to produce its television specials and films. After many years of working at Motown, she was no longer afraid of anything.

De Passe has described her ambitious nature as something special in her personality. She likes to go right up to the old, rich, and powerful people in Hollywood and say, "Okay, here I am."

De Passe realized that Motown, despite its successes, did not have the money "to push a button and make a movie." The money would always have to come from financial backers, wealthy people who were willing to take a risk on a new project. These people take that risk because they believe the project will make even more money for them.

Wisely, de Passe became friendly with Hollywood's upper crust. Her best friends still include Joan Collins, Farrah Fawcett, Ryan O'Neal, and David Niven, Jr. She goes horseback riding with actress and friend Anjelica Huston. She is a part of the Hollywood community.

When dealing with her co-workers, de Passe used all of her insight and native intelligence. One Motown executive has described her style of arguing topics with other executives: "As fast as they gave their objections, Suzanne tore their arguments apart. It was done without **hostility,** just naturally and painlessly. She's very clever, very quick, and can make instant decisions."

GETTING DOWN TO BUSINESS

When Gordy made de Passe president of Motown Productions in 1981, he gave her a development budget of $10 million. At first, she moved slowly and carefully. She produced another movie for her boss, *Berry Gordy's the Last Dragon,* and some television *Movie of the Week* projects.

Some of her early projects died in the making. De Passe knew, however, that this was part of the game. "There's a certain realism you must bring to bear at some point," she once explained. "Is the time you spend going to be rewarded—financially, emotionally, artistically? There has to be some payback, even if it's not financial."

Back to Basics

Gordy also told de Passe to put together a staff when he made her president of Motown Productions. She chose three women as her senior-management team. They called themselves "The Moettes," a joking reference to the early Motown female groups who had used "-ettes" on the end of their names (like The Marvelettes).

And it was early Motown that gave de Passe and her Moettes their greatest inspiration. Soon, in 1983, Motown would be twenty-five years old—a quarter of a century of hit-making superstars. Also, the date would coincide with Gordy's birthday. De Passe thought it would be a great idea to bring together all the great old Motown acts and have a gigantic musical celebration that would also be a television special.

Motown Forever

De Passe decided that her Motown special would serve another purpose. The five-hour event would also be a benefit concert for the National Association for Sickle Cell Disease (a dreadful disease that affects black children).

The new Hollywood mogul knew that her first major project as president of Motown Productions had to be a winner. De Passe decided that not only would she bring back many of Motown's great recording stars, but she would also reunite some of the groups that were no longer together.

Two of those groups were The Jackson 5 (with Michael Jackson) and The Supremes (with Diana Ross, Mary Wilson, and de Passe's old friend, Cindy Birdsong). All of her experience working with famous, talented people came in handy as de Passe struggled to pull together all the acts.

Making History

When *Motown 25: Yesterday, Today and Forever* aired on television in 1983, it was one of the most watched programs in the history of TV broadcasting. Although the original five hours were reduced to only two, the night was full of magic and surprises.

Michael Jackson appeared with his brothers and performed a medley of old Jackson 5 songs. The Temptations and The Four Tops held a singing "battle of the bands." And Diana Ross sang for the first time in thirteen years with former Supremes Mary Wilson and Cindy Birdsong.

To show the influence of the Motown sound on other performers, Smokey Robinson sang two of his songs with rock and pop singer Linda Ronstadt.

All of de Passe's hard work paid off. *Motown 25* was the highest rated musical special in the history of television. The show won an Emmy Award as Outstanding Variety Program of 1983. De

Passe won her first Emmy Award from the American Academy of Television Arts and Sciences for producing *Motown 25*. She also won a Peabody Award, an important award in the television industry, for the music special.

BACK TO THE APOLLO

In 1985, the Apollo Theater, where so many great black performers got their start, would celebrate its fiftieth anniversary. Although the theater in Harlem was run down and had been closed for years, there were plans to restore it. De Passe knew that this was a perfect opportunity to celebrate the reopening of the theater with another gigantic television special.

De Passe had always wanted to produce some kind of special about the Apollo. Now, her career had come full circle—back to the Harlem theater where she had stood in line to see the famous Motown acts of the 1960s. Still, she knew she would need some help with the project.

A Helping Hand

De Passe found that help in a woman named Jewell Jackson McCabe, the head of the National Coalition of 100 Black Women. McCabe was already working with New York's Inner City Broadcasting Corporation. This black-owned company had bought the old Apollo and was working on **renovating** it. Now, de Passe had to do some wheeling and dealing to get her special moving.

In 1985, the Apollo Theater, in Harlem, reopened its doors for a 50th anniversary celebration. That year, Suzanne de Passe produced Motown Returns to the Apollo, a television show honoring the theater where so many great black performers got their start in show business. She won her second Emmy Award for the special. (UPI/Bettmann.)

She and McCabe met with executives at Inner City Broadcasting Corporation. The two sides agreed that they would work together to create a show at the Apollo.

It is hard to believe how much time it takes to put together a television special. De Passe spent a year planning, negotiating, and—as she calls it—"hyper-begging" to get the show on the air. McCabe worked as the **liaison** between Motown and Inner City Broadcasting Corporation. Finally, the two sides agreed to do the project.

Getting It Together

When the special was completely planned out, Motown took the idea to the National Broadcasting Company. The network agreed with de Passe on one of her major points—the special couldn't be done in less than three hours. Thanks to her success with *Motown 25*, she was able to convince NBC that another Motown television show could hold its audience for an extra hour.

De Passe had one more ace up her sleeve. She knew *exactly* whom she wanted to host the show: comedian Bill Cosby. "That was the start of a major plot," she once explained. "It took about three months, with constant strategic updating—at that point his [television] series was on a **meteoric** rise."

Once Cosby agreed to host the Apollo special, other performers jumped on the bandwagon. They all wanted to say that they were there the night the Apollo Theater was reopened. De Passe would call the special *Motown Returns to the Apollo*.

Making a New Apollo

In addition to negotiating with all the managers and agents of the stars who would appear on the show, de Passe had to keep track of the Apollo's remodeling. It wasn't going to be easy to turn the historic Harlem landmark into its old glorious self after being closed for so many years.

Slowly, though, de Passe watched her old favorite childhood concert hall come back to life. "It was like magic," she has recalled. "Suddenly the molding was up and the paint was drying and the chandeliers were there." She couldn't help but remember how she used to tell her mother she was going to the library to study and then sneak off to the Apollo.

By show-time, de Passe had convinced more than 100 performers to appear on the special. What a galaxy of stars! Patti LaBelle sang with Joe Cocker. Boy George performed with Stevie Wonder. Little Richard sang gospel (religious) music with Al Green. And James Brown, the Godfather of Soul, brought the house down with his act.

That night was a powerful one for the woman who had grown up in Harlem and had stood in line to see shows at the Apollo. Now, twenty years later, she was riding in a long, black limousine to run a production involving hundreds of people. All of her dreams had come true.

"I got very choked up," de Passe remembers. "It was all those years, all that sweat and sacrifice, figuring it out and working and slaving and begging. All that stuff was worth it."

Another Success

Motown Returns to the Apollo, a three-hour NBC special, won de Passe her second Emmy Award, as the show's executive producer. This second success was an important one for both de Passe and Motown Productions. It created new possibilities and confidence in Motown.

"The second one said, 'It's not an accident folks; maybe these guys really know what they're doing and they've got something going here,'" de Passe once told a reporter. New projects sprang from her office.

A LEARNING EXPERIENCE

One of Motown Production's new projects was *Nightlife,* a late-night TV talk show that ran for 195 episodes. This television show was one of de Passe's most difficult. For one thing, it was filmed in New York, which meant that she had to go back and forth—constantly—between the West and East Coasts.

No matter how hard she tried, however, de Passe could not make working on *Nightlife* a pleasant experience. She has recalled that every change she attempted to make "was like trying to turn a battleship." There were too many problems on the set, the stage where the show was videotaped. Finally, the show had to be cancelled.

De Passe recognized her *Nightlife* experience for what it was—a learning experience. "I learned more than on any program I've done," she once explained. "That happens when things don't go right. It was a bitter disappointment, in the sense that when you work that hard on anything, you want it to work right."

Her next major project *would* work right, however. In fact, it would be one of the greatest successes of Suzanne de Passe's career.

Chapter 6

Lonesome Dove

In 1988, Berry Gordy sold Motown Records to another recording label, MCA, for $61 million. He took the profit and poured the money into Motown Productions. Suzanne de Passe would find special use for that money in the most unlikely place: a Western novel.

ANOTHER CHANCE MEETING

Three years earlier, in 1985, de Passe was in Tucson, Arizona, where she met an author named Larry McMurtry. They liked each other immediately, and she asked the writer if he had anything new she could buy the rights to (de Passe was always looking for new projects for Motown).

McMurtry told her that he was working on a new novel called *Lonesome Dove*. He didn't think she'd be interested, however, because it was a Western. "Well, all someone has to do is tell me I wouldn't be interested," de Passe has recalled.

After she convinced him that she wanted to read the book, McMurtry sent her 1,000 typewritten pages. The book had not been published yet. De Passe liked what she read. She felt the book was a modern-day classic about the old West. She knew it would make a successful mini-series on television. And it would be her biggest project ever.

At first, Gordy thought de Passe was crazy to do a Western, but he never told her so. "I never let on to her, because if something has never been done, that's reason enough to do it in my book," he has explained. Apparently, she had learned this lesson from her former **mentor.**

BREAKING DOWN STEREOTYPES

By acquiring the rights to *Lonesome Dove,* de Passe would prove to the entertainment industry that Motown could produce something other than rhythm and blues records and black TV shows and movies. She had learned this approach from Gordy, who always said that Motown should be "not black or white, but entertainment. Money is green."

"We handle everything," de Passe told the press, "and *can* handle everything."

De Passe paid $50,000—a very small sum—for the rights to turn *Lonesome Dove* into a television mini-series. Later, she found out that many large movie studios and all three major television networks—ABC, CBS, and NBC—had decided against buying the rights to the book. "We were sort of the last-chance saloon," de

Suzanne de Passe in 1989, on the set of the television mini-series Lonesome Dove. *De Passe co-produced the special, which starred Robert Duvall and Anjelica Huston and won seven Emmy Awards. Thanks to de Passe's wise business decisions, Motown Productions was able to buy the rights to the novel on which the mini-series was based. (Bernard Fallon and Columbia Broadcasting System.)*

Passe has said. "Motown was hardly the first place the manuscript was sent."

However, de Passe was the only one who had read the book and appreciated it. She could still recognize a winner—even in print.

Something important happened after McMurtry's book was published. *Lonesome Dove* won a Pulitzer Prize—an important award given each year to the best in American literature. Suddenly, the value of the book skyrocketed. De Passe had made one of the smartest business investments of her life: "God looks after fools, babies, and me."

Smart Business

At the time that de Passe bought the rights to *Lonesome Dove*, television networks would budget about $1.5 million an hour for a mini-series. After the novel won the Pulitzer Prize, CBS offered to spend almost $2 million an hour to produce the eight-hour mini-series. The network could now see that it had a winner on its hands. This meant that the project had $16 million of the $20 million needed to produce the expensive show.

Now, de Passe had some more quick thinking to do. She needed another $4 million. She found an Australian company (Qintex Entertainment) that was willing to buy half the profit Motown would make on the series for $1 million. In addition, the company would agree to pay the remaining $4 million in production costs.

A Gamble Pays Off

Therefore, before the cameras even started rolling on the project, which Motown had bought for only $50,000, the company had already made a profit of $950,000. And CBS and Qintex were paying for the production. De Passe has said that buying the rights "was a gamble in a sense, but we didn't bet the farm on it."

Lonesome Dove was a gamble that paid off. The eight-hour extravaganza—featuring more than eighty speaking parts—aired in February 1989. In the television business, February and May are known as "sweeps months." Network executives and advertisers watch what happens on television very closely during these months. Local stations set up their advertising rates—how much they charge a sponsor for air time—based on a show's ratings in a sweeps month.

Profit

> Profit is the money made after goods or services have been sold. It only costs $3 to make a compact disc, and a company sells it for $15. That's a $12 profit. Companies *must* make a profit to stay in business.
>
> When Suzanne de Passe bought the right to *Lonesome Dove* for only $50,000, she knew she had made a wise deal. As soon as Qintex agreed to pay $1 million for half the profit Motown would make on the mini-series, de Passe had made $950,000 in profit for her production company. That's smart business!

Lonesome Dove became the third highest-rated mini-series in CBS's history. CBS hadn't had a winner like that in almost five years. De Passe felt that the series' success was due in great part to the fact that they didn't water down the book for television.

"I think what *Lonesome Dove* has done is to say: Look, you can get the audience if you aim high enough. Not low enough—high enough," de Passe has explained.

An Award-Winning Series

In August of 1989, *Lonesome Dove* led the nominees for television's Emmy Awards with an incredible eighteen nominations, including Best Mini-Series, Best Directing, and Best Writing. Actors Robert Duvall, Tommy Lee Jones, Anjelica Huston, and Danny Glover also received nominations. That September, the mini-series won seven Emmies.

Lonesome Dove broke many of the **stereotypes** Suzanne de Passe had worked against for so long—stereotypes about Motown, women executives, blacks in television, Westerns, and TV mini-series. As she said at the time, her television blockbuster "put a dent in the theory that Motown Productions could only produce music or traditional black content."

Why did Motown make a Western? It was a question de Passe was forced to answer over and over again. As she told many reporters at the time, "I think people should be free to do and create anything that turns them on, and I think Motown Productions would be accomplishing a great deal if what our mold became was great entertainment. I say let's forget all the boundaries and let's just go for it."

Once again, de Passe had achieved her goal: *Lonesome Dove* had shown the world that Motown could do anything.

Chapter 7

Lady in Control

Today—many, many years after she stood at a New Year's Eve party and told Berry Gordy his company was mismanaged—Suzanne de Passe is respected as the woman who put Motown Productions back on top. She has become one of the most powerful executives in the entertainment industry.

Along the way de Passe has won a number of awards, among them: the Women in Film Crystal Award, the Equitable Black Achievement Recognition Award, the YWCA Silver Achievement Award, the Brotherhood Crusade Black Pioneer Award, the National Coalition of 100 Black Women's Candace Award, and the National Urban League Achievement Award. In 1990, she was inducted into the Black Filmmakers Hall of Fame.

De Passe also sits on the boards of the Los Angeles Chamber of Commerce, the UCLA Foundation, the American Film Institute, the National Urban League, and the Hollywood Radio and Television Society.

One of de Passe's Emmy awards sits on a table in her Los Angeles Office, next to the Image Award that she received from the National Association for the Advancement of Colored People (NAACP). De Passe especially cherishes her Emmy. "Because the statue is a woman," she says. "The Academy Award is called 'Oscar,' the NAACP award is a man, the Tony Awards are named after a woman, Antoinette Perry, but they're disks. I like the Emmy."

AGAINST ALL ODDS

In many ways, it has been a long, hard climb for de Passe. As a black woman, she has had to overcome many obstacles, not the least of which have been both **racism** and sexism. But she never let the odds against her get her down.

"At the end of the day you can't let the stats [statistics on racism and sexism] overcome the tasks," she has explained. "You can't be more invested in the details of what those odds may signify than you can in your own ideas. It's not that you never notice those things, but it's how you handle them."

As de Passe once said, "It's been very sweet to see the expressions on people's faces when they realize I'm the boss. They understand black women singing and dancing and acting. They understand black women sweeping and ironing. But they don't understand a black woman telling them what to do."

Being a Realist

In addition, de Passe is a realist. She learned from Gordy that *money* is the real issue in any business. As she has said, "The greatest racism in Hollywood has to do with what color ink you produce. Black or red." When a company is losing money, they say it's "in the red"; when it is making money, it's "in the black."

"It's one time that black is considered very good," de Passe has explained.

De Passe was also lucky to have one person, Berry Gordy, believe in her and guide her through her career. Still, she has remained her own woman. "I consider myself a product of Berry Gordy, but not a clone [double]," she points out. "He and I are always friends and colleagues, and I will always revere him as a mentor and boss. Though, of course, I'm always struggling for more *equal* footing."

When Gordy first brought de Passe to Detroit, he told her: "This will either make you or break you." There were many times when she thought it was going to break her. She has even said that Gordy was more of a "tor-mentor than a mentor." But nothing ever stopped her; she rose to every challenge and met it head on.

HOME MANAGEMENT

Suzanne de Passe lives in a California-style house on the same street as actors Jack Nicholson, Warren Beatty, and Marlon Brando. Since 1978 she has been married to an actor named Paul Le Mat. Le Mat is famous for playing a teenager cruising in his pickup truck in the movie *American Graffiti* and for many other film roles.

For their first date, Le Mat surprised de Passe. He took her boxing, but he never told her that *he* was boxing that night. Le Mat says they have a special relationship, although they are very different: "Suzanne likes fancy clothes, I don't. And she likes limos, which I'm learning."

At first, de Passe was worried about the problems some men have marrying a successful woman. "Unlike a lot of other men I dated, Paul did not suffer from competition or jealousy. He has a total acceptance of me and what I am doing. He's been 100 percent supportive," she has said.

De Passe has said that the two lead a relatively normal life and often stay home. "Couch potatoes," she adds jokingly.

LOOKING AHEAD

For Suzanne de Passe, the road from working at the Cheetah disco to becoming president of Gordy/de Passe Productions (formerly Motown Productions) has been a long and exciting one. Her life is a lesson in taking chances—in believing in yourself and working hard. Nothing has ever stood in her way.

With de Passe leading Gordy/de Passe, the world can expect more successful projects from that production company. She knows the power of an idea. "There's always a creative idea flying through my mind," de Passe once explained. "I wish I had the time to work on all of them. Every time I need a good idea, God gives me one. And that's a nice resource."

Glossary

assembly line An arrangement of machines or workers in which work passes from point to point in a direct line.
choreograph To arrange or direct movements, as in a dance.
discrimination Treating someone differently on a basis other than merit.
entrepreneur One who organizes, manages, and assumes the risks of a business.
ethnic Relating to large groups of people according to racial, national, or cultural background.
hostility Hatred or ill will.
idiosyncratic Odd or oversensitive.
liaison One who helps to maintain a close connection between two parties.
meteoric Like a meteor (shooting star) in speed or in sudden brightness.
mentor A trusted guide; a teacher or coach (a mentor's student is often called a protégé).
mogul A person of power.
persistence Continuing to do something despite any problems.
persuasive Capable of changing other people's minds.
racism A negative attitude toward others based on their race.
renovate To renew or restore to former life.
rhythm and blues Popular music mixing blues and Afro-American folk music.
stereotype A mental picture about someone or something that is too simple and general.

Index

Academy Award, 35, 58
Apollo Theater, 19, 20, 21, 45–49

Beatles, 14, 17, 29
Birdsong, Cindy, 8, 23, 25, 44

CBS, 54, 55
Cheetah (discotheque), 22–23, 29, 60
Cosby, Bill, 47

De Passe, Suzanne,
  ancestors, 20
  awards received, 35, 45, 49, 57, 58
  childhood, 20–21
  education, 20–21, 22
  marriage, 59
  and music, 21, 31–32
  parents, 20
Detroit, Michigan, 12, 27
Dreamgirl: My Life as a Supreme (book), 29

Emmy Award, 44–45, 49, 55–56, 58

Ford Motor Company, 12, 13
Four Tops, The, 7, 13, 14, 44

G.I.T. on Broadway (TV special), 34
Goin' Back to Indiana (TV special), 30
Gordy, Berry, 8–17, 19, 23, 25, 27–28, 29, 31, 33, 34–35, 37, 52, 57, 58–59
Gordy/de Passe Productions, 10, 60

Harlem, New York City, 19, 20, 45, 48
Holliday, Billie, 35
Huston, Anjelica, 42, 55

Image Award, 58

Inner City Broadcasting Corporation, 45, 47

Jackson 5, The, 29–31, 44
Jackson, Michael, 30–31, 39, 44
Jones, Anthony, 30

Lady Sings the Blues (movie), 35
Le Mat, Paul, 59–60
Lonesome Dove (book and TV mini-series), 51–56

Mahogany (movie), 35, 37
Manhattan Community College, 22
Martha and the Vandellas, 14
Marvelettes, The, 14
McCabe, Jewell Jackson, 45, 47
McMurtry, Larry, 51–52
Moettes, The, 43
Moonwalk (book), 31
Motown Productions, 9, 10, 17, 34, 39, 41–50, 51, 56, 57, 60
Motown Records, 7–17, 21, 23, 27–28, 51
Motown Returns to the Apollo (TV special), 47–49
Motown 25: Yesterday, Today and Forever (TV special), 44–45, 47
Movies, distribution of, 37, 39

National Association for the Advancement of Colored People (NAACP), 58
National Association for Sickle Cell Disease, 43
National Broadcasting Company (NBC), 47, 49
NBC, *see* National Broadcasting Company

63

New Lincoln (school), 20–21
Nightlife (TV show), 49–50

Oak Bluffs, Massachusetts, 21
Oscar, *see* Academy Award

Peabody Award, 45
Pulitzer Prize, 53, 54

Quintex Entertainment, 54, 55

Racism, 58
Richie, Lionel, 29
Robinson, Smokey, and The Miracles, 7, 14, 19, 28, 44

Ross, Diana, 16, 17, 33, 34–35, 39, 44

Sexism, 32, 58
Sexual discrimination, *see* Sexism
Stereotypes, 52, 56
Supremes, The, 7, 8, 12, 13, 14, 16–17, 23, 25, 29, 33, 34, 44
Syracuse University, 22

T.C.B. (TV special), 34
Temptations, The, 7, 12, 16, 33, 34, 44

Wilson, Mary, 14, 29, 44
Wiz, The (movie), 37, 39
Wonder, Stevie, 14, 18